I0027111

The Unconscious of the Consciousness

Redeeming Ourselves

James Qeqe

The New Voice of Africa

Edited by Emmanuel Mabelane

PUBLICATION
CONSULTANTS
We Believe In The Power Of Authors

PO Box 221974 Anchorage, Alaska 99522-1974
books@publicationconsultants.com—www.publicationconsultants.com

ISBN Number: 978-1-59433-966-0
eBook ISBN Number: 978-1-59433-967-7

Library of Congress Catalog Card Number: 20209439147

Manufactured in the United States of America

Dedicated to
HE +Thabo Makgoba and to the
Archbishop Thabo Makgoba Development Trust

Foreword

Africa you are on your own!

Just like a mother who is left on her own by an irresponsible father to raise her children, this is the very same situation in which Africa finds herself today. Just like a woman who has been raped, violated and abandoned in the bushes to bleed and die by her perpetrators, so is Africa. Just like a first born child who is an orphan, left all alone to take care of her younger siblings, consumed by hunger and poverty, so is Africa today. As much as mothers who raise their children on their own always triumph and make sure that they raise giants, children who will stand, defend and take care of their mother as she grows old, in the same way, the children of Africa must rise, defend and take care of their Mother Africa.

In as much as the women who are raped and become powerful and living testimonies about the possibility of healing, these women become 'wounded healers' these women empower their fellow brothers and sisters, these women restore the moral compass in their communities, so must the children of Africa rise and ignite the torch of Africa morality. Daily in Africa, we witness and hear triumphant stories about child-headed homes/families, although is tough and emotionally draining, an African child always rises against all odds, against all calamities, so must Africa rise today against the seed of division which was planted by colonialism, a seed which is being watered by blood of the children of Africa.

There are many bad/evil seeds which are foreign to Africa, it is painful to see our people irrigating and consuming the fruits of such seeds. It is time for the children of Africa to rise and uproot such evil seeds, xenophobia, sexism, Gender Based Violence and racism among many. The children of Africa must go back and dig deep into the wisdom of their ancestors because they have embraced the western way of thought. It is high time for the children of Africa to consult with those living ancestors who are "Afri-conscious," those who hold Africa's interest at heart and learn from them in order for the children of Africa to be able to rise, defend and protect their Mother before the second wave of "Scramble for Africa" demoralizes her further. James Qeqe is addressing these issues, and many others. His voice should be

heard, and all other voices that cry out the same pain should indeed be heard. AFRICA ARISE!
(Mthokozisi John Mthombeni 17th June 2020)

Which Way Africa, Which way Africans?

27th April 1994 is rather a day that most South Africans would never forget, mostly those who suffered from the hand of the oppressor during the dark era of Apartheid in South Africa. It is the day which all South Africans had waited for all those years. Finally it came. This was to be a new beginning for the country, and the question was, 'what next?' this question and many others had to be answered. Because it was the new era that had washed away the old in which our people had been teargassed, brutally tortured, bitten by the police force and dogs, and struck with quirts and batons.

Many people waited until they were too old to vote, the likes of Archbishop Emeritus Desmond Tutu was sixty-two years old when he first casted his very first vote, and the president of the new Government of National Unity Mr. Nelson Mandela was seventy-six. Many did not live to see that day. One can imagine the exuberant feelings, fears, anxieties and even excitement that was prowling around the country. But at the same time, anything was possible, it was in the hopes of South Africans that, 'never again would people be uprooted from their homes to be dumped as if they were rubbish in poverty stricken Bantustan homeland... Never again would God's children be humiliated by the crude methods employed by the Race Classification Boards as they sought to separate South Africa's inhabitants by race as if they were cattle.' (Tutu 1999: 15)

What is it that we are doing wrong? Or what is it that we are not doing at all? How can there be so many sufferings in the Mother Continent after so many years of struggles, and eventually Independence and Freedom were obtained by the heroes and heroines of our great land of Africa. Like in the 1970s as the Irish were asking 'What can we do?' when the height of their riot season in Northern Ireland arose, the Troubles, as it was known. So we too, Africans should ask, 'what can we do?'

Let's look at Dr. William Nkomo of South Africa, who had been one of the founders and became the first President of the militant African National Congress Youth League, is recorded as to be one of the prominent leaders of our times. He was a spokesmen of the South African 'unusual' group that visited Northern Ireland. To help the Irish in their struggles. The unusual group included white farmers, ministers of the Dutch Reformed Church and black headmasters. So it was thought that if the Irish were no longer prepared to listen to each other, perhaps they would listen to South Africans. Do South Africans listen to each other now? Do Africans listen to each other perhaps? A story is told about Dr. Nkomo. One day he was driving in his home city, Pretoria. Not realizing that some roads had been rerouted for a civic occasion, he drove the wrong way up one-way street. A white policeman, quite rightly, stopped him, but then began abusing him and finally hit him in the eye. That reminds me of Dr. John Kani as well. Nkomo then took him to court. Just before he was due to leave South Africa for Europe the case came up for trial. The policeman was found guilty but discharged anyway.

Why am I reminding you about this story? Simply because we are still doing the very same thing that were done to us by our oppressors. We even add to the oppression. Here is an example, today in South Africa, and in other African countries as well. A person would kill another, and be arrested, in few days or so they are released, they are free. Not that they were not found guilty, but because they have rights, they are free, they are independent. Are we not saying to them, continue the evil mission? Are we not fueling the fire of cruelty to the nation? Should we not be also charged for not saying anything? Tell me, are we in the right path to success,? To development?

In our societies someone is raped at least every week, but no one gets arrested, if there are, they are released. Very soon than expected. Haven't we taken too much to God? Mustn't we take this to blood? I am not proposing war, hear me well.

I do not only speak on political perspective, but on moral obligations too. I do not just speak of political choices, vital though these are. I think, rather, of how people react in a pressure situation, their motives, compulsions and their aims. These I think, will decide what system evolves.

But where is the world heading to? The Soleimani assassination, of Iran? Is that the relationship we want with other nations? What does it reflect? Mankind's capacity to destroy itself has become a commonplace. In the coming years it is possible that some dedicated or unbalanced guerilla group will get its hands on nuclear weapons and use them regardless of consequences. You have only to shut your eyes as you hear men and women of Southern Africa, and of Africa at large express their honest feelings and you can picture yourself listening to Protestant and Catholic in South Africa Black and White in South Africa. French and English speaking communities of our decent, Australian and Aboriginal and so on and so on. The list is endless. Maybe it will have more effect if put in ancient version, the Jews and the Gentiles, the circumcised and uncircumcised, the rich and the poor, the educated and the uneducated, again, the list goes on. So allow me to say, we face a universal need to rectify the wrong doings.

I am writing this, in a moment of reflection as we begin the year 2020, remembering the giant President Julius Nyerere of Tanzania, being reported as saying, '... it preferable for anyone to live in a country ill-run by his own people than well-run by someone else...'. One comprehends his point, but trust me, we would be in a very devastating moment if that would be the only alternative. On the other side, for a white man, there is another dilemma. Which could be the fact that he sees Communism's bid for his country and rejects it. But mere anti-Communism serves the communist purpose.

Many people ask, 'Which way will Africa go?' I am aware that Africa has been through a lot, and that there are developments successfully archived. But Africa is rather confused, there is a crisis in character. I am saying this because, men who were united when they fought for the freedom of their continent and countries have now allowed self-interest to take precedence in their lives. Is that what they were aiming for? Is that what they wanted? Unless we can get an incorruptible type of leader who will not be bought with money, with position, with fame, with success and with promise of other things, then Africa would be doomed. The natural self-interest of great powers adds to this. I think we need a new ideology, the ideology that begins when a man listens to God.

Two thousand years ago, a man called Paul put it nicely, he wrote, "My own behavior baffles me... I often find, I have the will to do good, but not the power. That is, I don't accomplish the good that I set out to do, and the evil that I don't really want to do I find I am always doing... it is an agonizing situations. I thank God there is a way out."

I wish that we come to discussions on what change do we want, what kind of Africa are we building. I am saying a discussion because it may happen that the Africa that I want is the Africa that you don't want. And that will lead to a conflict, and that will lead to another, and another and another. It's time to wake up Africans, it's time to be in the forefront and take our own decisions, that will Africa forward that will make the next generation proud of us.

The Zimbabwean, or the Rhodesian?

Prof. Peter Hannon notes one of the greatest events in the soil of The Rhondesian and The Zimbabwean. An unusual gathering emerged, as the students of the coloured University of the Western Cape jammed into their biggest hall, at the expense of their lunch time. The attraction? Good question! A mere announcement came up saying that Rev. Arthur Kanodereka, Treasurer General of the African National Council (Muzorewa wing) and Alec Smith, son of the Rhodesian Prime Minister would speak. I suppose the mood was tense, as the story is told. A great number of the audience were men of passion. Some on the other hand had been imprisoned for the strength of their opposition to South African system. Interesting enough, official student policy was one of no contact with the whites.

All together, wanted to know what this unusual combination would have to say. What on earth could bring the son of a white Prime Minister and the representative of the Black Nationalist movement to speak on the same platform? What was the catch? Who was selling out? Prof. Hannon says that Alec Smith spoke first. Still in his twenties like many in the audience, he went on to the offensive. He was not there to defend or justify Rhodesia. I think he was not in a position of defending it either. He was there to challenge the students to join him in building a just society. Then Rev. Arthur Kanodereka was introduced. He is a senior man, middle-aged unlike Alec, with the grey hairs of experience. So he says... "I know what violence is. I have lived up on the North East border of my country and have supported the guerillas there. I have seen white men killed and black men killed, and looked at their bodies. I know what oppression is and what it is to suffer. I have been arrested three times by the security forces. But I have come to see that why bitterness was also imprisoning me. That bitterness has now gone. With it has gone any spirit of submission or inferiority. I am now a free man." Bitterness is all that could have destroyed his life, like Dr. William Nkomo, realized that bitterness had made him a prisoner, limiting his vision and distorting his fight. Like Smith, Kanodereka told his audience facts of change in hardcore whites and blacks. He said it was a totally new factor in his country and that it strengthened the black man in his fight. He himself could meet

anyone without fear. That is what we all want. To meet
anyone without fear. A friend of mine in class was asked
a question if they ever felt intimidated and inferior in
the presence of a white man. "Yes." He said. I don't want
to come to any conclusion, but that really hurt me. That
someone would be intimidated just by a mere presence
of another. What have we really done? Was our black
skin the wrong we ever did? We never crated ourselves;
it was the Almighty who decided this skin on us. It's
time that Africa wakes up. And this time it should mean
business. I am not for whites, neither for blacks, but for
all humanity.

I regret to share this story with you. One time I
was traveling to Cape Town City, South Africa. When
I landed, I drove in an Uber from the International
Airport to Maitland. As we stopped in a traffic light, I
noticed that across the road there were three children,
they were all girls. Two of them were black, and one
was white. They were intending to cross the road, by
the traffic light, but they were scared to do so. I guess
because of their ages. They were age seven or eight by
the look of things. One black lady came to their rescue,
but only took the two black young girls and left the white
alone. I thought she would come back again to take the
other one. But she continued with her journey. The
white little girl was stranded as she did not know what
to do. She was left alone. The other two black girls were
still waiting as they wanted to go back to their friend. As
I was looking and reading this situation, another black

woman came and took the girl to join her friends. They were all happy after all. That is my South Africa.

I might be wrong or what so ever, but I know I am not. Racism does not only apply to black people by whites. I personally believe that all races are racist, but some races are more racist than others. Which sound like the seventh commandment in the book entitled 'Animal Farm' by George Owel. I am saying this because I have seen it live, races rise up against each other, and you'd find out that whites are no were to be found in the picture. So I am saying racism is not only on white palm of hand, not that there are no whites who are racist anymore, but it's not always the case. South Africa still suffers from this demon, which we haven't found any good exorcist to exorcise it. I refuse to be treated inferior because of the colour of my skin. Over my dead body. These are the matters that young Africans should engage and talk about. These are the matters that are destroying the Mother continent of Africa. Again what should be done?

Kanodareka did not only act on the level of national affairs. Fresh truth grew up in other spheres. You would swear that much of his forcefulness today springs from what has happened in his family. His hate of the white man had spread into his home and damaged his wife and children. He found that you cannot control hate. Especially if you are not putting any effort. He called them together and told them he was sorry. It was not an easy step, but I guess it renewed his family. Sorry!

Sorry! Sorry! I wish any offender in the future would learn how to say these words. Sorry! Sorry! Sorry! They don't make the one saying them a coward, but a hero and a heroine who knows that they were wrong, instead the make them the best amongst the best.

While still in Cape Town City, in a Taize Pilgrimage, chilling with friends in the Marist Brothers' house, after a midday prayers led by the Taize brothers from France, we were also privileged to have His Excellency at his old age Archbishop Emeritus Desmond Tutu of the Anglican Church, and his predecessor, His Excellency Archbishop Thabo Makgoba, with His Excellency Archbishop Stephen Brislin of the Archdiocese of Cape Town of the Catholic Church. I received a message that I was summoned by a group of people to a meeting.

"Are you James Qeqe"? The messenger asked.

"Yes, who wants to know?" I replied.

"I am here to let you know that you are needed in a boardroom, there is a meeting there, you can only find out then." The messenger said as he was departing from my sight.

I did not know what to do, or how to respond at least. I decided to leave for whatever meeting I was summoned to. I went to the boardroom, and to my surprise the room was very somber, and you would swear that someone had died. Everyone looked at me as I was entering. I did not even greet, as I pulled out a chair and sat. Was I wrong for not greeting? Maybe I was, as an African child I should've known better. But no one would blame me, I was confused, by the look of things the meeting seemed too serious.

I was then welcomed by the gentlemen who was chairing the meeting. He was a Ghanaian judging from the accent and looks. He then rehabilitated the purpose of the meeting. It was after the recent so "called xenophobic attacks" in South Africa, dated 2019. I don't know why I was called to that meeting, but I went anyway. For the fact that I came to a pilgrimage did not count, neither did it prevent me from going to the meeting. As they say "curiosity killed a cat." The meeting was about the matters that are holding back Africa from growing. To count few, the xenophobic attacks; the economy crisis; and even corruption by African leaders. The boardroom was filled by Youth African leaders from some parts of Africa. Zimbabwe was represented, Zambia, South Africa, Mozambique, Namibia, going up north, Ghana, Nigeria, Kenya, Tanzania. Malawi and Botswana were also present. To my surprise, there were also few from outside the continent. China, Italy and even France were on board. I thought this meeting was for Africans only.

The first person to share in the meeting was a Zimbabwean. He was very anxious about the Zimbabwean matters. I was crossing my fingers that he does not talk about the 'Zimbabwean Economy Crisis'. I know, that is a very long conversation, we would have not finished, even today, if we start to talk about that, we would not finish. It is a very sensitive matter, which is not a one day tournament. The Zimbabwean was concerned about the xenophobic attack in South Africa. "When South Africa experiences xenophobia, there arise a division in Zimbabwe." The division is between the Shona speaking people, and the Ndebele speaking people. When I follow the story precisely, the Shona speaking people do not regard the Ndebele speaking people as to be Zimbabweans. Now what do you call that? How do you address that? Or who has occupied whose space?

So when South Africa experiences xenophobia, the Shona speaking people in Zimbabwe attack the Ndebele speaking people, for they say they do not belong to Zimbabwe, but to South Africa. After he has address the house, he sat down. So by the look of things, that needed a South African to answer. That needed me to answer. No one else would have answered that. Why? Because I was the only South African in the room. That was for me, and knew from the beginning that if I failed this, I'd be finished.

Before I was given a platform, a Nigerian gentlemen requested to pose a question. He was granted the mandate. So he asked, "Can someone give us a brief history of the Ndebele speaking people, and the Shona speaking people?" he then sat down, and I was left to answer those imposed questions.

The Shona speaking people were under the hand of King Dehwe of the Mwene-Mutapa kingdom, also called and pronounced 'Monomutapa'. While the

Ndebele speaking people were under the hand of King Mzilikazi, also known as 'Moselekatse'. Both have been found in the land of Zimbabwe. It was during the Mfecane Wars that the Ndebele speaking people settled in north of South Africa and south of Zimbabwe. Because King Shaka kaSenzangakhona, of the Zulu kingdom wanted to absorb the small kingdom of the Ndebele people to be under his rule, and would emerged with the mighty Zulu kingdom and become one. But Mzilikazi did not want that, he was too protective, so he was flying around the country, and eventually around Southern Africa and landed in north of South Africa and south of Zimbabwe. During that time, the land was not divided, it was known to be one region. When the Europeans divided the land, they never considered those, neither did they care who was were. But it happened that some Ndebele people be in South Africa, and some in Zimbabwe. Now how do you solve that problem? Who do you put the blame to? Are they not one people? Speaking the same language and practicing the very same cultural customs, ceremonies and activities...

At least they were pleased by the answer I gave. But the Nigerian not being satisfied, he pose another question, which I feel like it was more provocative than seeking understanding. So the question was... "Why were South Africans attacking the Nigerians in the 2019 xenophobic attack?"

I must be frankly honest with you, I needed to be awake than I was. That question was an honest question, it needed some clarity and more explanation. The Nigerians in my understanding believed that the attacks where between them and South Africans. But the attacks were not xenophobic, I am not saying this because I am a South African, and that I am protecting South Africa. The recent attacks were not xenophobic in this sense, the people who were attacking were not attacking people who come from outside the country, but criminals. Criminals who are killing and destroying young lives, by selling drugs to young ones, attacking drug lords, prostitute lords and all that. Again I am not saying that it was fine to attack. Taking the law to their hands was not right and cannot be justified. But they felt like the police were slowing down the pace. But let me be clearer. In South Africa we do not have a group of people who attack Nigerians because they are Nigerians, nor attacking Zimbabweans because they are Zimbabweans. That group in South Africa does not exist.

The Chinese and the other guests from Europe and Asia also talked about corruption. They told us that they are aware of corruption taking place in their countries, and they want to address the matter. Which made me think, why Africans should wait until they get invited to America, Europe, Asia and Australia to talk about their problems. Why can't we Africans talk about our problems first? I applaud to them, simply because they had guts to talk about corruption and yet we Africans are scared to talk about it. They however advised that we talk about it amongst ourselves, and thereafter do something about it. Now that meeting was over, I thought to myself... 'I was privileged to be part of that meeting'.

Let me divert a little bit. One day I was walking in the streets of Pretoria, where I happened to pass a couple of students, (university students) who caught my attention by the topic they were battling with. Apparently these were classmates, maybe friends too, these were Black South Africans, from different cultures and spoke different languages. The topic that they were battling with was to ask each other 'what is the name given in their respective home languages to xenophobia'. I thought that was a million dollar topic. In IsiNdebele? They didn't know. In IsiZulu? 'No'. Xhosa? 'Nothing'. Sepedi? 'Nada'. I heard to pretend that I was on the phone call so I stood no far from them were I could hear them properly without them noticing that I was listening to them. The reason I did that was to respect them and their privacy in the topic. They don't know me, neither do I know them. But I was hoping that at least someone was going to give an answer, a name to this. But no, no one gave any name. Because if someone had given the name, then we would have translated the name to other languages, that was my aim. But dololo ukuphuma igama. Ndantsho ndancama!

Which taught me however, that xenophobia does not exist in Africa, as it is reported in the book 'The

Unknown of the Known in Africa', that this is not part of our history, not part of our cultures, not part of our languages either. So where does it come from? A bit of research that I did on this, was that the name itself is foreign to us. It is of Greek origin, and Romanized version of it 'xonos' which means 'stranger' or a 'foreigner'. And 'phobos' meaning 'fear' 'phobia'. So this is actually the 'fear or hatred of a stranger or foreigner'. Now tell me when you see Africans together, who foreign to who? Who is a stranger to another? Where is this coming from? Who brought it? Who painted this on Africans? For what? Since when did Africans begin to distinct themselves in their languages or cultures? Africans in the past had spoken their home languages with one another without needing any interpreter or translator. They could understand each other, but they would not be able to respond with the same language. So you would literary have two or more people speaking each one in their own languages. How fantastic is that?

How have we missed ourselves as Africans, and allow ourselves to be dismayed by a nonsensical approach that was painted to Africans, probably by non-Africa. How educated are we to be misled by such nonsense.

Africa is ours and We are of Africa:

I am recorded to have said the following speech, which was inspired by that of President Thabo Mbeki of South Africa.

WE ARE AFRICANS

We are Africans-Black or White by James Y Qeqe 'The New Voice of Africa).

Cultural Day 08 September 2018

Rector of the seminary, Very Rev. Father Paul Manci, Vice Rector of the seminary, Rev. Father John Selemela, Father Deans,
Formators of St. John Vianney Seminary,
Teaching staff and non-teaching staff,
Representative of the foreign cultures.
Our distinguished and domestic guests.
The sons who are the descendants of the great King Moshoeshoe-the Basotho people.
The sons who were led by Sekhukhune Barota or BaPedi people.

The representatives of the Zulu land, the sons of the Mighty Zulu throne of Sigidi Shaka kaSenzangakhona,
Batswana people. The Igbo's of the Nigerian's community, the Ghanaians of the Asante, the Tanzanians, the Coloureds, led by Adam Kok III, Swati representatives led by Mswati Mavuso II, The Ndebeles led by Mzilikazi.
CapeTownians .
Ndingabalibelanga abantakwethu from the house of Phalo, kaRharhabe, right through the house of Gcaleka and Ngub'engcuka, the Xhosas and abaThembu of the Eastern Cape.
AFRICANS AT LARGE,
Dear Friends.

In such occasions, we should, perhaps, start from the beginning.

So let me begin.

A wise man once said and I quote, "No man is an Island, he was conquering and yet became a wise African man who once charged 'Umntu ngumntu ngabantu'- moto ke moto ka bato- a person in and through other people." When I saw you in the traditional attire I heard myself saying, 'indeed when "Greek meet Greek the struggle becomes titanic.

To be an African for me it means everything, it means I have a home, and that I do exist. It also means that I belong, that I have life, and that I am proudly African.

I am a black person, yes! I am black, because 'I am an African' and black is beautiful.

As former President of the Republic of South Africa Mr Thabo Mvuyelwa Mbeki once said in his speech in 1996- "I am an African...I am born of the peoples of continent of Africa,... it feels good to be an African." The black skin does not mean shame or rustiness in the inner person, but it means you are a person being recognized amongst the peoples. Let us then imitate our forefathers, our heroes and heroines, such as Hinsta, Moshoeshoe, Mpande, Mzilikazi, Mswati Robert Moffatt who brought peace in our land. And those who existed in our time, people like Steve Bantu Biko, Martin Luther King Jr. Malcom –X, Stocky Carmichael. The iiNdlovukazi of our times Mariam Makheba, Rosa Parks, Albertina Sisulu, legends such as Nelson Rholihlahla 'Dalibhunga' Mandela, Thabo Mvuyelwa Mbeki, Frederick Douglass Washington and many more.

I am the great-grandchild of the warrior men and women that Phalo, Rharhabe and Sekhukhune led. The greatest that Mswati Mavuso II took to battle. The peacemakers that Moshoeshoe and Mzilikazi including Hintsa taught never to fight the unnecessary battles.

Do not reluctant to express yourself as an African Black or White. And remember this, you're not recognized as who you are, but as what you are. 'The black skin is not badge of shame but rather a glorious symbol of national greatness'.

We are no longer separated, as Blacks or Whites, Indians or Colours, but now we are united as Black and White. Africa belongs to all who live in it, there is no African foreigner in an African country, all Africans belong to all African countries, and all African countries belong to all Africans. "WE ALL GOD'S CHILDREN" and "MY HOME IS YOUR HOME" and that means we are one. We all make mistakes because we are human beings, it is important then to learn from them. LET'S LET BYGONES BE BYGONES.

Belike like children, because children do not carry baggage from one day to the next, they start afresh always. African be proud of who you are, White or Black, Colored or Indian. We are ONE, one we are, because we are one.

I am not better than you, we are just the same. Let us treat each other as brothers and sisters, who share the same AFRICAN BLOOD.

May we with a contrite of heart heed the call to repentance and be the sign of God's mercy and compassion to the world. Amen!

My culture is your culture, and your culture is my culture. There's no culture which is superior to the other. I can teach you something, you can also learn something from me, and together we can change the world.

Happy cultural day.

Ngiyabonga,Ke a leboha, Enkosi, Ndiyabulela, Danki, Asante sana, Ngiyathokoza, Ke a leboga, Ndi a livhuha, Ndza khensa, Dalu, Natotela sana and I THANK YOU!

My Village Life

I was never so dedicated to anything than my village life. I was so passionate about it and that it taught me a lot. I could not exchange it with anything, I am no better to anyone. I believe everyone is clever at their own discipline. I entirely object to the idea that there is someone superior or special on earth. I need proper conviction to make me buy that. Many old men in the village have asked me many questions, but only one question have stayed with me till to date. "Why do you sleep alone?" or "How can you sleep alone? I will give you one of my daughters..." That is the funniest and yet embarrassing question to answer. Not that I cannot answer it, but to answer that to an old men is more uncomforting. Of course they would never allow me to sleep with their daughters, not before I pay the Lobola. That's not how things are done in Africa. Not in the villages. But that was a call for me to look at their gardens and see their beautiful flowers sprout up in the sunny day. It was a call to take one of their girls when I am old enough to get married. The saw me as a gentlemen, as a man amongst men. Most of the time they would say this, "I wish you were my son. I wish you were my child." I never understood what they meant, until to date. At some point they taught maybe my life was fantastic and easy. No! Oh! No! It was not! Maybe it was, until my father decided to marry another woman who would become my step mother. That was in 2004 when they got married. My mother died in 2001, I was still young, but cautious and alert. We never said to my father we want another mother. That was myself and my sister. We wanted to be where God wanted us to be. We were just fine with the people around us. We did not want a stranger not that age at least. But we were too late. They got married, at some point we were excited, and on the next we were scared. We kelp on asking questions. "What kind of a person is she?" "Will she manage us both, plus her husband?" "Does she even have a heart?" And all those nasty questions.

But my experience with my step-mother is one I would not wish even upon my worst enemy. I was abused, physically. Most of my days with her were those of tears. My step mother always pretended when her friends and family was around. Especially when her husband's family was around. That is why they kept her trust. She was loving in their sight, she was probably the best thing ever. I don't blame them, they never lived with her.

I visited a friend from another village, and had gone out with them to a little ravine where they dug clay for the potters. Using little hoes, they filled skin sacks with the little lumps of hard clay they had dug up and these they eventually dragged all the long way back to the village. Although that was a women's work, but we were fascinated to learn how to do it. Their husbands were the potters who sat inside the houses and huts making pots and so forth. I needed a break from home. I went away, and on my way back home, I felt like something was off loaded from my shoulders, thank goodness we had no phones those days. I was relieved. Only if I knew that my step-mom was waiting for me to beat the hell out of me. That was her job, to beat the hell out of us. We never find time to go out with friends, we were always busy at home with unending house chores. Most kids in the village had house duties, which they would do every day after school. But this was unbearable. Ours would take forever until it's even late to go and play, and socialize with other children in the villages. It was even worse during the Easter Holidays and during festive season, when knew children are in the village. By the time you are allowed to go out and play, probably for only two hours, all other children know the new ones.

One day, my late cousin Mpiri visited us with her young daughter. They only came to spend the day with us. It was a Saturday morning if my memory serves me well. My step-mom was using a Siemens, one of the old brand cell phone. My step-sister, still very young, took the phone to play games. I tried to confiscate it from her, but she would cry. And when she cries the world stops. I must be honest, I wanted to play games too. I was bored, not allowed to go and play with my peers. But I let her play with, it was her mother's anyway. She did not know what she was doing with the phone, she was just pressing as many buttons as she could.

It was after some few hours, when I noticed that my step-sister had abandoned the cellular phone, and went to play with our cousin outside. Finally, the phone was all mine. Until I got hold of it. It was blocked to my surprise. The worst part of it is that she appeared (my step-mom) while the cellular phone was in my hands. I bet she had concluded that I was the last person to have the phone. My sister did not know that the phone was blocked. She just could not press it that's all. I could not wait for Mpiri to leave us, so that I face my trial once and for all. I was not hoping for any mercy. I was ready to carry my cross and move forward. Even if my step-sister would be found guilty of the phone, still the blame would be on my shoulders. Where was I when this all happened? I was not going to defend myself, I was just going to surrender. Just like that. I was tired of this, nothing was interesting at all. My life was not boring, not at all, but I lost interest of it, that's all. I tried and tried, but nothing.

So Mpiri, my cousin left, and no the battle of the blocked phone was on the move. There was going to be blood on the stage.

"Yamkela!" she called, unhesitant.

"Mma!" I responded. Gulping air heavily.

"What happened to my phone? It's blocked."

"It was your daughter, she was playing games remember?"

I should have not said that. I just should have not. The thing with her is that if she is ready and had activated her mind to beat someone, forget, it's already done. Just ask one question, 'who will it be. So as I thought, there was blood on the floor, and I had to wash dishes while bleeding. I so wish that Mpiri was there, just to see the everyday life I was assigned to live. Simply because they praised her, they loved her to bits.

Anyway, I was more fascinated by the potters' skills. Of course the skills I have learnt from the other village. The potters' methods were very simple. They sat on the ground inside their huts and turned the pots on small round chocks with a stud underneath. They worked the chocks with toes, which are as sensitive and prehensile as fingers, and achieved a fine speed. I spent most of my time as a boy with old men of the village. Some of them said that I remind them of my grandpa, who died in 1997. Yes! I know him. His name was Simon Qeqe. We look alike, they would say. Some even believe that I was Simon incarnate. Well I never felt like like I was Simon at all, I always felt like I was James. Every time

I had to introduce myself as James, son of Michael, son of Simon. I still want to believe that, if my grandfather was still alive things would have been different. I don't know, it's only a thought. I was fascinated when people at school told me about their relationships with their mothers. It was really amusing, until I get enough of it.

Things became worse when we moved from KwaMavuso location to Bhalasi location, near King William's Town, where my step-mom was born. By the way, the Mavuso location was named after chief Mavuso of the amaBhele clan. Believe it or not, my mother was from the royal family, and I was also a Mavuso before a Qeqe. That changed after she passed on. Yam-Yam as she used to call me. Only Emmanuel Mabelane calls me that, I wonder how he knows about it. To my mind, only people close to my heart called me that. When Emmanuel calls me that, it's equivalent to my mother's. Anyway that was just a pass by. When we moved to King William's Town, things became worse. Yes, we were now far from the rest of the family, and anyone could do whatever they wanted with us. I hated the life at first. Everything was new, like literary everything. New friends, new family, new school, and new church new everything believe me. That's also when I converted to Catholicism. Well that's a story for another day. All of a sudden life in the new village was bit different, but more chores now, and guess what more oppression. I wondered where God could be in all this situation. But I always had a prayer in my mind that if God can be with the Israelites and take them out of the land of Egypt where they were slaves, would He not do the same with only two people? My sister and I? Surely if He could do that with hundreds of thousands of people, and have them same until the Promised Land, would He not do that with us? What changed? Of course time. But what was my sin to God that he was so slow to hear my prayers? Was I never faithful to Him? Or was it my mother's sins that I was paying for? What went wrong? I could not bear the look at my sister's face. It was too much for me. I was hoping to die, it was hard. At school you would even wish that it doesn't go out. But phike? It was my life, it was mine and mine alone.

On the other side, my father was there, he would not say anything. Many said he was finished by his wife. I could not argue about that, by the looks of it, it was true. My father was too protective towards his wife, to such an extent that you would not say anything bad about his wife. Oh! Not in his presence at least. But it was what it was. We used to talk about anything with my father, but not in those days. I even regretted why he got married. I wish I was dead at once not to experience all that. At some point, both of them were not grateful. Most of the boys at my age, when their parents start abusing them, even if they were not abused, but, would consider otherwise. They would go and do drugs, womanizing around and all that sort of a thing.

Could they not spare me at least? Could they not give me credit for that?

Many people have crediting with the title of being wise, some would say intelligent. Which I always doubted. I was never cleaver, not at all. If they want to know, they must ask Ms. Madikane my English teacher, or even worse Mr. Galawe my Math teacher. I was just a coping guy, which I am still am.

The Chris Nenzani I know

It was in 2010 when I first encountered Mr. Chris
Nenzani, personally. I have known him for many years
before that, and apparently he was famous in the local
area, but what was he famous of? No one would tell. I
guess it's because he was a strict man. Very strict. Such
that if you didn't know him personally, you would con-
clude that he was cruel. During those years again, still
in the lower grades of the secondary school in which
he was teaching. I became his right hand man, who had
an access to his office at any time when needed. He
was a Deputy Principal, for almost two decades until
he was elevated and promoted to a higher position in
another institution. It was in Bhisho High School near
King William's Town when I met him. He was a History
teacher. Now you can connect the dots why we became
friends. We always talked about history, most of the

time we met. Remember I was not a cleaver learner, nor a fast learner. But he liked me a lot. "For my effort" to know more as he would say. He liked to make a joke of me in class, for writing more that the maximum pages in my history essays. That didn't make me the highest in class, but I was not failing at the same time.

Before he was given a post at St. Thomas, a Catholic School, where Fr. Luvuyo Madikane is currently working as a priest, our Vocations Director in the Diocese of Port Elizabeth. There were rumors about Chris Nenzani, that he would be something bigger that the Deputy Principal. We all wondered what he could be. A principal maybe? No! He was not going to be a principal, Mrs. Majerman was still healthy to continue for another decade or so, she was still young to retire too. Everyone in school was asking me about this new post that Mr. Nenzani would occupy. Especially my classmates. They asked me because I was the 'right hand man' of Mr. Nenzani. I was not his secretary, but an assistant with the assembly organization. Every time when we had an assembly gathering, Tuesdays and Thursdays, unless there could be a special assembly or that a very important visitor from the Department of Education, from any respected place, then I would be in charge. I would go to Mr. Nenzani's Office, at any time. Sometimes just to check up on him.

I have known his wife before him. She was and still is in the Parish Finance Council, as a member. You can say she is a Treasurer General of the Parish of St Rose.

I worked with her for many years, as I was the Parish Council Secretary. We sat meetings together, compiled reports, grafted year plans and all that. It was during that time that Mr. Chris was converted to Catholicism. I was there to witness it. It happened in one evening that I was watching news after finishing my home work. It was reported on that evening on the news that Chris Nenzani and other delegates were in the Eastern Cape Legislature. It was there were I did my training to be a Public Speaker. What on earth were they doing there? At that time of the evening? I then received text messages and phone calls, mostly from my classmates, asking me about what they've seen on the TV. To my surprise, I did not know that my classmates were watching news. It was a shock. They were asking... "What does Mr. Chris doing in the Legislature?" I had no idea what was Chris doing in the Legislature. My classmates thought that I was hiding something from them. I was not. I swear to God, and to my mother's grave. Chris never shared anything with me about anything of that nature. It was later announced on that very same evening that Chris Hubert Nenzani was elected new President of the Cricket South Africa.

That was really unexpected. It was a wow moment. Our History teacher, was now the new President of CSA. So again, it was merely two minutes after the South African Broadcasting Commission made the announcement, I again, received phone calls and text messages, telling me that, "So this is what you have been hiding all along?"And another, saying, "You're good in keeping secretes. Well done!" and another, "So Chris did not come to school for three days, because of this. Wow congratulations to him." And many others which I cannot remember. I was not looking forward to go to school on the following day. I knew, it would have been a topic of the day. It was going to be James in the middle of it. I did not want that. I just wanted to go to school like a normal child. That's all. Exactly as I had thought it to be. When I entered the classroom, they all applauded me. As if it was me who was named the President of CSA. It was Chris' not mine. It's him they should applaud for. Anyway, Chris returned to Office after two days or so.

The Deputy President of the Learners Representative Council, (LRC) Mr. Sive Dingiswayo was one of those who came to see me to ask about this new post that Chris was now appointed to.

A big announcement was made in school, by the principal. We were all in fascination. It was really a well done. From that day, I didn't know how to address Chris. He was still the same Chris, but no man. I held the keys to the Office of the new CSA president with me. All along. But it was really a no big deal. Chris was still the same. Who wanted his homework and assignments to mark and pass or fail us? His history though was rather tougher to some of us. It was like Math. Most learners did not like him in class, but outside class, oh yeah, that was fine. I wanted to resign as the assembly organizer. Why? Not because Chris was now the president of the CSA, but I had too much on my plate. I was an actor at the Department of Education under Mr. Litha Makasi, one of the former South African actors, who is famous as 'Diliza' in the South African Drama Story known as 'Kwabakwazidenge' (Hill of Fools) in English. I was a debater at Steve Biko Foundation, sponsored by Forte FM Community Radio. Oh! Yes, I was also a PPC Secretary in the Parish of St. Rose of Lima, under Fr. Peter Chungu-Shitima. Again, I was the Secretary at the Deanery of King William's Town under Fr. Gabriel Muyenga, at that time. I could not take it anymore. Again, I had too much to do.

I told Chris that I think we should find someone else to do the Job. Mr. Chris asked for a reason. I told him that I had a lot on my plate. Chris would not listen. Every time I would start this conversation, Chris would interrupt with another topic. He always changed the topic, every time I was raising things. I knew, he did not want to lose me from his Office. He wanted me to serve there until I finish. I guess I needed to do that. Don't get me wrong. I enjoyed working with Mr. Chris Nenzani, I gained a lot of leadership skill, and I had gained confidence that in whatever you do, do it out of your best. That was the type of a leader I wanted to be. Like Chris Hubert Nenzani. He was inspiring, intelligent, and self loving. If you were not from Bhisho High School, and came to Bhisho High School meeting Chris Nenzani, you would swear that he was the principal. Not because of the size of his body. But because of himself. He was huge, a giant. But that did not make him more of an important figure. Although it did, but he never intended it to make him one.

In his presence, you would feel intimidated. He is tall and big at the same time. At school, there were guys who would carry knives, because they were them. But not to Chris, Chris organized an Operation Gqogqa, to search for knives in the school. And if he finds you with the knife, either in your pocket or bag, he would call your parent, only to tell them that you were suspended, for having a knife in your pocket, in fact for bringing it in the premises of the school. He was then called 'Mabhozo' which is slag name for a knife in IsiXhosa. Every when Chris would come, whether in class or wherever, learners would say "Mabhozo is coming." Or this one, "Hlalani phantsi, ibhozo liyeza." Which translates "Take your seats, the knife is coming." Indeed the knife would come. But the tendency now was becoming. We were getting used to it such that we would forget that, that was not his name. I always wondered if he knew the name, as sometimes in the office I would be tempted to call him. But I would always remember and stop myself. Many teachers also knew the name. And many teachers respected Chris, and would listen to Chris more than the principal. Chris didn't like that, he always emphasized that he was not the principal, but the Deputy of the Principal, an assistant in other words. The thing about Mrs. Majerman was that she was too soft. She was very slow in taking decisions, but believe me, whatever decision she would have taken, would probably be the best of them all. It is funny enough that at school Chris Nenzani was my boss. But in the church I was his boss, as I was the secretary of the Parish Council. He would report to me for the matters of the church, and I would report to him for the matters of the school. But in all those, we never disrespected each other, we never went to each other's toes. We still respect each other, I still visit his house, he's still my history teacher, I do some of my researches with him. He's still a faithful Catholic, committed. We meet at Church, and chat about anything. He is one man, amongst the very few I really admire, not for the work he has done, but for being a hard working machine who never allowed it to affect his personality. Even to date, many teachers at Bhisho High School regret his appointment at St. Thomas as the Administrator. According to the things have changed, a lot. I remember also when I was still under him, Arnold Kalipa and Sidney Tyakume accompanied me to his office, and we were the first one to complain to him about the teenage pregnancy. And that year it was the highest number in the history of the school. About twelve learners out of close to a two thousand pupils were pregnant. We needed to address the matter, and as an additional member and adviser to the SRC, I called the meeting to talk about the matter. I want to believe that, since Chris left, things have changed. Nenzani reflects the through kind of leaders that we need in Africa, leaders that listens to people, leaders that are not occupied by their high offices, leaders who serve their people, and leaders who are not little kings and mistresses.

The Hot seat in the Secretariat Office

Many people I met and those who wrote to me, who have read the summary articles of sections of this book said to me that, I must be 'very brave' to write about my experience in the secretariat office at Saint John Vianney Seminary, Pretoria, South Africa. As a matter of fact, I don't regard it as to be a matter of being brave, but an unavoidable burden and load of responsibility. I have been a secretary before, it was not my first time, surely neither it was my last. I am recoded as to be the first Student Council Secretary to come from the lowest class of first year Philosophy. I don't know, that's what they say. I am happy to have opened the doors for others, because my predecessor is also from the same class. I might have fears and be anxious about sharing or telling this story, but the fears are real and the consequences dire, but my conscience never dispel just as it never dispelled during my service as the secretary.

Believe me you, my disposition towards taking my faith in God seriously does not help in this regard. Instead it compelled me to do what all of us would really want to avoid – maybe take a risk that could change have an enormous impact one's life, future and career. I never took anything to myself. Neither was I a civil servant. I never wanted to be regarded as a hero, but just a mere servant to assist where I could.

On the 03rd October 2018, still doing first year philosophy, I was elected the new Student Council Secretary of the Student Body at St. John Vianney Seminary. According to the constitution, no one can reject any of the positions if elected, unless one has a 'valid good reason' not to. I wondered what could have been a 'valid good reason' not to accept the post. I honestly did not want to accept the post, for only one reason, I know how it feels to be a secretary, I know the challenges, I know the lot of work, and above all I know the intimidations. As noted above in the preceding chapter that I have served in the PPC as its secretary, and in the deanery as well. For about five years serving on both those high posts. I always knew that I was young to do that, but I did it anyway. I pushed as at time I felt like I had no choice but to do it. My processors Mrs. Mchiza was very much helpful. As I would often go to her for some clarity and other information. As expected I was to write minutes of every meeting we sat, but it did not end up there, I was expected to translate they in three languages of our deanery, that would English, IsiXhosa and Afrikaans. My Afrikaans was not so good, I always asked someone to do it for me, or at times just leave it and not do it. The Afrikaans speaking understood, I was not ashamed of it, not at all. I was also too busy to learn another language. I was literary too busy to do so.

Serving as a secretary under President Sipho Given Mavimbela was one of the best ever experiences. I had two diaries in my office, his and mine. I kept a full time diary for him, but not just him alone, I kept a full diary for the entire SC members, as I would often send emails to them as to remind them of what would take place next, according to our year plan. I enjoyed doing it, tiring as it was. I am also the first secretary to own an office. In whatever years. But don't think that was an impressive move to others. Yes to some it was. But many criticized the move. That's when I saw that I won't last as the secretary, I would have to resign at some point.

President Mavimbela like any other president was a favorite to some, and was a threat to others as well. I knew from the beginning that I ought to play my cards as clean as I could. I am aware on the other side that it was not going to be easy, as I was faced with challenges already in my office. It was some midnight when I first received some note pads with writings "resign", "you're not the president", "you think that you are the president" "we never voted for you" and many others. I had a choice to take the notes to the president, and to the rector himself. But I did not. I just did not want to do it. The notes were printed, they were not a hand written, which could have been easier to trace. I was not in the mood to entertain all that nonsense, I was worried about my studies, and the new task that was assigned to me by those who trusted me. It was mostly my classmates, who voted for me. We were the biggest class. Yes some from other classes also voted for me, because I won the vote with absolute majority. But the biggest influence was done by the Philosophy 1 class. President Mavimbela respected me, not as his secretary, but first as a human being. The respect was mutual. He is a kind person who does his job without doubt. He was very slow in taking any decisions though, because he had to think on everything that comes to his mind. But the decision that would be taken there-after would be probably the best. Nevertheless, many people have said things about me, some of the things were said in my hearing, but I guess others were said to my friends or those who were close to me, as they would often tell me that this is what they think of you. I thank God I had no time to be going around the seminary confronting people. My philosophy is that I wait for battle to come to me and then I would respond to whatever is directed to me. Some saw me as a coward, it was fine. I mean I was in the seminary for God's sake, a place which was supposed to be holy and peaceful. I was not there to be a politician, I went there to study to become a priest. That was the ultimate goal. Nothing less nothing more.

I told some of my friends that I was planning to resign with the immediate effect, Mitchell Cloete who had been the Sports Entertainment Coordinator Officer (SECO) in short. Mthokozisi Mthombe, Obakeng Masetlha and of course Nathi Mabelane. I was going to resign midnight 16th May 2019, I was in Port Elizabeth to attend Fr Runaine James Radine's priestly ordination. Mabelane knew about it. As he was the only one who knew at what time I would be resigning. Even before I left, he came to my room a night before I would have resigned. He stopped me, and told me every reason I probably wanted to hear not to resign. I was not failing in my office; there was a lot on my plate. Some of which were family and personal issues. I was going to send the letter to the Student Council by midnight on that day. It was going to be fine, because I was away from the seminary; I was in another province, in the Eastern Cape. I was not planning to cause any drama that is why I wanted to resign in my absentia. The president together with the SC had decided the 17th May 2019 to be the day for the Student Body General Meeting. I had typed all the necessities such as the minuets of the previous meeting, the quarterly reports and the Agenda published in all seven notice boards in each block in the seminary. I wanted the president and the SC to announce my resignation in the general meeting, and if needed be, elect another secretary in that very same meeting. I had it all planned in my mind. Fr Hendrick Montgomery suspected something about my behavior in the ordination as he had attended. He is a friend of Fr Runaine from Keie-mos Upington. He was my friend too.

I did not tell him what I was thinking, because I knew what he would say and do. He was probably going to phone the president, former student as he was, still was capable to do so. But because of Mabelane I did not resign that night. I did not forgot to, but he asked me not. Not to please my enemies at least. I am glad I did not. At least I finished my course, like St Paul I finished my race. Few months later, a similar incidents happened. I had an argument with one Brother from Durban, which ended up being serious and to an extent that we would suffocate one another at each other's armpits. I phoned Emmanuel that night, I was about to sleep. His room's window was opposite mine, so I looked through the window, and I noticed that his lights were already off. So he was sleeping. I then decided to write a note and had it slide under his door, to read whenever he wakes up. He woke up thirty minutes after I have slid the paper under his door. I was shocked. He came to support me. He was there to cry with me. It's not that it would have been my first time to resign. No! I had resigned before. It was at Steve Biko Foundation, when I was accepted as one of the new actors in the field. I was happy, excited. But I felt like I was called to go to the seminary which was the ultimate thing I ever wanted to do. So I received a call from the Vocations Director to tell me that I was summoned to the bishop's office. I was to be shown my new office by the CEO of that time, Ms. Obenewa Amponsah, and other directors. Actually acting has been my thing ever since I was a child. It was my own, I lived it. It was after some few auditions and meetings. Prepared and unprepared auditions with big bosses of the foundations.

On the Thursday of that week, I was to go to my new office, it was the 25th February 2016, and on the very same day, I was expected to see the bishop in his office. I must say, I was left between a rock and a hard place. I had to resign as the PPC Secretary as well. And I handed over my resignation letter to the daughter of our chairperson Mrs. Ngaso. She asked her daughter to drive me to town, to meet Fathers Luvuyo and Runaine. She accepted my resignation immediately, she wanted this for me. I had to make a choice, I had to choose. It was not easy, I then wrote a letter of resignation with immediate effect. I was aware that many of them would be worried and sad. Devastated in a way. I was now on my way driving to Port Elizabeth City, ready to receive all those phone calls text messages and emails to tell me that I must be joking. I was together with Fr Runaine, then still a seminarian and Fr Luvuyo the VD. I had to answer some of those phone calls, some of those text messages and emails to confirm that it was not a joke at all. I had made up my mind, I was also hurt. It had to be done anyway. Those were the people I was starting to get used to, knowing them better. But it had to be done, in one way or the other.

I do not like to disappoint people, simply because I know the felling, I do not like to be disappointed too. But they had to work on getting someone to replace me, I know that it was not easy to get someone to feel my shoes. My shoes rather were rather bigger than anyone else's. Eventually, someone had to feel up the gap and continue. Resigning at St John Vianney would have been no different at all. Like the retirement letter, or the 'End of Term Letter' that I wrote sounded like it was a resignation letter. As it read:

October 3rd 2019

Dear Mr President,
Deputy President,
Master of Ceremonies,
Colleagues,
To all members of the Student Council,
Chairperson of the IEC,
Members of the IEC Executive,
Dear friends,
Seminarians,
Brothers in Christ,
As you know that tomorrow, October 04th 2019, the Student Body will elect the next President and his co-workers, that is to say: the Student Council Executive and Student Council leadership at large, of our respective institution, Saint John Vianney

Seminary. Who will then swear his and their oath of office on the same day or few days later.

By law and bound by our Constitution of the Student Body, I will therefore cease to be Secretary General of the Student Council, by midnight today. I thought I should write this letter as one of my last communications to you as part and member of the Council of our seminary's leadership.

First of all, I would like to thank you all, for having finding me worthy to occupy one of the most difficult positions in the rank of the council. The Secretariat Office. I am saying 'one of the most difficult positions' because of experience in the past. To the president and the council at large thank you for having agreed to serve in the Student Council and Student Body when you were requested to do so. This demonstrated your selfless commitment and dedication to serve the community of St John Vianney Seminary, which told me that I was privileged to have the possibility and opportunity to work as part of such a collective of dedicated individuals.

All of us seminarians in leadership, together, have always understood that as members of the Student Council, and other committees we carry the heavy responsibility to stand in front lines of our community charged with the dedication to achieve the goals to better our lives in formation and ultimately in the Church. I assume that we all

know, by definition, all changes are not, to quote
the giant Nelson Mandela, enhanced by another
giant Thabo Mbeki an 'easy walk to freedom'.
Accordingly, our own continuing change has not
been, and is not, and will not be an easy walk to freedom. That is to say an easy walk to success. It will
constantly test and pose a challenge to everybody,
including ourselves, to prove through our deeds,
rather than our words, that we are true change
makers and true servants. This will demand that
we walk the long and hard road to achieve a better
goal. Always conscious of our obligation to serve
the people, rather than promote our own personal
interests. As tried and tested combatants for the
victory and consolidation our aim to better our
lives and formation as matured future priests. You
have had no need for an instructor to educate you
about the challenges we would face and face, time
and again to achieve the objections in bettering our
lives. Your decision to serve in the Student Council
has therefore meant that you are willing to walk a
hard road that would necessarily demand personal
sacrifices. It is for this reason that I thanked you
for your conscious and voluntary agreement to
join the Student Council. I thanks also those who
have voted us, who have entrusted us with these
humbling tasks, because that says to me, that they
have seen something that would change the current situation in the present environment.

In this regard I must emphasize the fact that the charge given to the Student Executive Council through all the years of our formation, mandated by the Student Body through fair elections, has been nothing but to pursue the goal to bettering and educating ourselves for future purposes. I make this observation in part to pay tribute to you for the loyal and principled manner in which you have consistently and consciously approached your responsibilities as true servants of God. With immense pride, I would like to convey to you my firm conviction, empirically demonstrated by life itself, that you have indeed honored your responsibilities to our seminary and formation, as mandated by the Student Body.

At the same time, I am certain that during our period in leadership we have served as the members of the Student Council we have made mistakes. I am equally convinced that the only way we could have avoided these mistakes would have been if we had done nothing to strive to achieve the fundamental social transformation of our community. In this context, as true servants, we must at all times remain open to criticism and self-criticism, precisely to ensure that we identify whatever mistakes might have occurred and correct these.

At the same time, I am aware of the reality that there are people, who in authority are known as successors would be open enough to correct these mistakes, as we did with our predecessors.

I make these comments, at this particular moment, to reemphasize the value system that has informed all of us as we served in the Student Council, concerning our quality as individuals charged with the responsibility to play a leading and exemplary role as leaders of our community. In this regard, and in the end, the ultimate motive power that would inform and has informed our behavior as individuals are our conscience and self-respect, individually.

Please convey my humble thanks to all the members of the Student Body, those entrusted me with this humbling task, and to all those worked in our Independent Electoral Commission of SJV (IEC) in preparations for our Oath taking.

I bid you all a fond farewell as a member of the Student Council. Because we have become brothers, friends, and partners in pursuit of a common cause, I trust that it will be possible for us informally to continue talking to each other and one another, concerned, still, together to serve the people and the community of Saint John Vianney Seminary. I promise to be at assistance where needed, and to my successor who would occupy the seat in the Secretariat Office in few hours.

Yours in Christ,
James Qeqe.

The Claws of the Cat

I Love my country South Africa. Some hate it. Most of those who live there and most who look at it as outsiders would agree that change is really needed and is bound to happen. The same is true for the neighboring countries, and many other far off countries as well. Thinking of Zimbabwe among many others. An unanswered question is: what kind of change will it be? Or what kind of change do we want? To choose between, for or against a certain group or that group, is rather facile. I come from South Africa, so I have no basis for self-righteous judgment of any country, whatever the rights or wrongs. In our country South Africa, in our cities, lanes and streets, bombs and bullets, knives and kidnappings, killings and maimings are the price we pay for unanswered prejudices and hates. South Africa is still divided, it has two societies, the rich white society and the black poor society. I am not saying this because I am a black South African, but because it's a reality that every honest human would unceasingly testify to it. It is the very need of countries like my own which makes me want to write about Zimbabwe and other countries, for I believe it is possible that from tip of this vast continent there could be mined, not just gold or uranium, but something of even greater value the cure to that which divides man from man.

I agree, that is a bold thing to say. There are few places where such divisions are experienced. I love Zimbabwe, is a nice country with lots of loving people. I remember travelling from South Africa to Zimbabwe. We had a meeting while I was still an actor. To represent Mr. Makasi's Association Group of Actors. I had to catch a flight to OR Tambo Int. from East London Airport, and another from OR Tambo to Harare, Zimbabwe. When we landed in Johannesburg, waiting for another flight to Zimbabwe, we received some phone calls and emails from the Zimbabweans, to tell us that we must postpone the trip to Zimbabwe because of the Zimbabwean xenophobic attacks. It was in 2014 if I am not mistaken. South Africa is in a brink of war. As I remember thinking about it, a pall of smoke hangs over Soweto, in Port Elizabeth, killings are becoming chillingly commonplace when rioters roam the streets. It was devastating as you would think of it.

In the plane I boarded in East London to Jo'burg, I was seating next to a Zambian. He was scared because the xenophobic attacks were on another level. As a linguist, I learnt some few words of ChiBemba language, which he spoke. And I shared few of IsiXhosa with him. He insisted that I teach him as much words and phrases as I could before we landed. I did not understand why. But he explained to me that by the time we land, he wants us to speak IsiXhosa, so that the perpetrators who might be in Johannesburg may not take note of it. Selfish as I was, I wanted to speak more of the ChiBemba language. But luckily enough, nothing happened.

I am sharing this to say that most people live in fear in South Africa, because of the instability of others. Many are innocent as they are all painted with the same pain and brush as to be corrupt and evil of the crimes committed in our country. There are many people who are to be blamed for this. Many of our own kept quiet because they benefit. Take this from me, in South Africa we there is no group that attacks Nigerians because they are Nigerians. Or whatever nationality. I mention Nigerians because they are always the 'victims'. We need to understand that our country's stability depends on us, on those who live and love it. We need to come together and address these and other matters. But I gain what should be done?

During the Angolan war opinion polls testified that the sympathy of most South African blacks lay with the MPLA. This did not mean that they were pro-Communist. Their instinctive support, however, went to those who "were teaching the white man a lesson." So how does the white man find a role which does not disarm him, but which will enable him to take an ideological initiative, rather than always be its victims? Another is: How can the white man, a tiny minority in a black continent, move beyond resisting for as long as possible the inevitable pressure of a vast black majority? He may do it for a generation. But, on that basis, what future can he offer his children and grandchildren? Or maybe in Peter Hannon's version, "How can we be sure that the oppressed, when he comes to power, does not in turn become the oppressor, thereby perpetuating the exploitation of man by man? White and black face two further questions. Is the black man, in his determination by those who will use him for their own, quite different ends? One hears voices which say, "Our aim is to create a Marxist state!" 'One man one vote', or wishes of the majority of their own people seem to take second place in such people's calculations. Their interest is power. Nothing else but power. Where one might hear himself asking, does that differ in motive from their picture of their picture of those they want to overthrow.

Speaking of overthrowing... I am aware that there were people who wanted to do so. While I was still a secretary of the Student Council at the seminary. They wanted to overthrow me simply because they were scared of change. That was my problem being in the leadership, people are afraid of change. But how can we grow if we can't submit ourselves to change? How can we develop our society if we are not open to explore? Is that too difficult? I heard many people in our SJV community most of them being seniors of the seminary that is to say the theologians, or students who are in theology classes, whether Theology 1, 2, 3, 4 or 5, as they would say, "we have got the seminary in this position, we shall leave in the same position. I am not a rebel, but trust me, that's nonsense. We can't live on what does not grow or develop the community. We must try and get another method or formulae. Emmanuel Mabelane uttered the words, "We all have a deep longing for peace, but who's got the correct formulae? Then the fighting begins."

My step-mother

One day, it was during the mid-year examinations, just after our exam, I went to her as she was standing alone waiting for her friends to finish up writing. Hi! I said. "Hey" she responded.

"You're beautiful as usual." I said. She couldn't say anything about that.

"Tell me about yourself" she said smilingly. I didn't know where to start so I asked.

What do you want to know about me?

"Everything! Where were you born, and grew up, those kind of things" She said.

I don't know where to start.

"Come on! Historians always know where to start."

She had a point there, historians always have something to say. So I said. I was born in Pretoria, in Mamelodi. But after few weeks after I was born, my mother took me to Alice were both of my families orig-inate from. I am the first born and only son out of four sisters. We're only two from my biological mother, and other sisters have their mothers. I grew up in Alice in a Royal family under Chief Mavuso. But later moved to my father's family. My family. My mother passed away in 2001 and I grew up under a step-mother.

"How was it growing up under a step-mother?" she interrupted.

"You don't want to know, trust me." I replied. But she insisted. I guess in one time I had no choice but to give her answers she wanted. "Be honest with me" she concluded.

At that time I wasn't comfortable talking about my experience, it was too much for me, concerning what I have gone through. It was... it was too heavy, I didn't know where to start.

'Please James, if I am not asking too much'.

After my mother's funeral, my sister and I were taken to my father's family where we belong. Because we were still little, my father entrusted us to his sis-ter, our aunt. She became our mother. Veliswa Qeqe her name. She took care of us, and to be honest we didn't feel motherless but she covered that. My father was working eBhisho near King William's Town. He only came back on weekends and on public holidays. Few years later, he took another wife who became our stepmother.

'Ok...!'

Few days after their marriage, that was in 2004, my father then entrusted us to her, traditionally that's how it should be. When a man gets married if his children are young then the new wife becomes the mother to them. She was nice to me, all the time. More especially when she had visitors. She called me "Yam-Yam," "Boy!" And sometimes he would call me "Son" and all other pleasant names you may think of. I loved that, I guess every child needs that. After few months she began to change, or rather I became aware of what she really was. She was antagonistic towards me.

"Antagonistic!" She said.

I have to tell the story again, please pardon me.

You have no idea. I remember one day, my late cousin Mpiri visited us. May her soul and all the souls of the faithful departed through the mercy of God rest in peace. Amen. She was with her small baby girl Unathi to come and play with Hlumelo the first born of my stepmother.

'You mean your step-sister?'

Yes!

There were also other cousins of mine and children who came to play with them. I was so happy to see the house so full with children, it was a while since I saw everybody. I was a prisoner at my own home. She kept me from seeing everyone. I only saw my friends at school, those who were not schooling with me, I hardly saw them. I could see from her eyes that she was not pleased at all to see her house so full with my cousins.

But of course she didn't want to make that obvious to my cousin Mpiri. What really she was.

What happened then? Babalwa asked.

She had a Siemens phone, my little cousins took it and played games. I took it from them, and played games as well, as she was having a conversation with Mpiri in the bedroom. My little cousins wanted the phone back, and that I was kept busy, so I gave it to them. Apparently they blocked it. And it couldn't work anymore. Seeing that it was blocked, my cousins put it on the table, and left it there. They went outside to play some of the indigenous games. I wondered why they all went outside. They enjoyed that phone game. I was happy because I was to take the phone to myself and play until I get tired.

Immediately when I put my hands to it, she came out to the pantry and saw me having her phone. But she didn't say anything, she went back to the bedroom and closed the door. The phone was not working, it was blocked. I quickly went outside to them.

What did you do to that phone? I asked them. But I didn't get any answers instead everyone pointed at each other. I knew what would happened to me about that phone. I could feel it in my blood. Mpiri was still in there with her. After hours, it was then early evening, Mpiri and cousins left us. Now I could finally say, I was alone again. I didn't want them to go. Few minutes after they left, she asked for her phone, I pretended as if I didn't see it.

"But you had it during the day!" she said.

'Oh! Yes, I remember now.' I said. I went to the family room to look for it. It was there under the coffee table. I took it to her. I gave it to her and immediately I went out to my room.

She called me!

"Yamkela!"

Ma! I responded.

"Come here!"

I knew what would happen. I knew exactly what would happened! It was in my blood. I swore to God and to my mother's grave... with my eyes closed.

"What did you do to my phone?"

It wasn't me. I swear. I said.

That was a wrong answer, to her if you said you don't know something you were telling a lie, even if you didn't.

What happened then?

She beat the hell out of me, she beat me up like nobody's business. My nose bled and there was a pond of blood in the kitchen. She left me there, and had commanded that I wash the dishes instead of crying. I washed the dishes and I hadn't stop crying, with my nose still licking blood as an unclosed tap. It wasn't the first time though, but I kept it as a secret.

Yhooo! What!? Babalwa said with shock. Why didn't you go to the police station or at least to your family? She asked.

And do what? Report that I was abused? Physically abused?

Yes!

No one would've believed that. Everyone loved her, and she was so sweet to people in general. Besides I didn't think of that. I was still young. I tried to say this to my family, but they doubted what I was saying. Only Veli my aunt whom I talked about early would sense truth in what I was saying. But the rest. No!I didn't say anything to my father, he wouldn't believe me either. He loved his wife as much as he loved me. I also didn't want to be the cause in their separation although that would've been the best thing for me.

When my father came on weekends, she would be very nice to me, and call me "Son" "Ndoda"and all that, pretending as if everything was fine. I really wanted to tell my father, but I couldn't. As thousand years to God are like a day, to me a week was like a thousand years. I only got a little of freedom on weekends.

'This is very sad.'

As we were still talking one of her friends Mihle came by.

'Why are you both looking sad? She asked.

Sad? You're mistaken, you should get your eyes tested. I said.

'I know what I see. Anyway I would like to talk to Babalwa, if you don't mind.'

Not at all. I'll see you later. I left them there. It was almost History period for me, and I should think it was Economics for them.

'The Rise of Soviet Russia. Who was the Tsar during the Russian Revolution Litha? Mr. Nenzani asked. Tsar Nicholas II Sir. Litha Zanekile answered.

Litha Zanekile was one of the cleverest leaners in the class. There were at least a number of people who were cleaver in our class. Counting few...people like Litha Zanekile, Zukiswa Pityi, Lindokuhle Mbabela, people like Khanya Dubula and so on and on. Khanya Dubula was a great Historian, there was no one who could beat him in that, and even his researches were the best. Even myself I could not get to his level. But I always told myself 'one day is one day.'

'From which year did the Russian Revolution took place?' James! Mr. Nenzani asked again.

From 1918 to 1939 Sir! I was so lucky to be asked that question. I guess it was an easy question. It may be easy but that's what make history to be so tricky to have all the dates of different periods and events in your head. But to be honest, that's one of the things that makes a person to be a good historian.

'Who was the name of the Priest who led the march of workers to the Tsar at St. Petersburg and what was the name given to that day and why Khanya?

'It was Father Gapon Sir, the day was called the "The Bloody Sunday" because of the blood in which the Tsar ordered his solders to kill the workers including Father Gapon.'

'Very good! That means you've studied. All of you, I am proud of you. Thank you Twelve B.' By the way, our class was known as Grade 12 B. Only two classes did History in Grade twelve, it was Grade twelve B and Grade twelve E. To Mr Nenzani's eyes we were always the best in History compared to Grade twelve E. in fact most of our teachers had approved that and jealousy had prompt out. There was this competition now, which was not a bad thing, not at all, because it was motivating us as leaners. After learning about what Father Gapon did for the Russian people, I realized that as the leader sacrifices should be part of your priorities. I mean Father Gapon led the people to the Palace of Tsar Nicholas II to march for difference, and he was in front of the workers, and became their voice. But that didn't end there. He was one of the first to be killed for change. To me he knew what would happen there, but still he had courage to lead the people forward.

So as I predicted beforehand what would happen in having her in the house, like Father Gapon, I had to be courageous and lead my siblings, especially Nandi whom I call 'Twin sister'.

'...but what is more painful is to love someone and never find the courage to let that person know how you feel...'

Babalwa and I became best friends, like nothing else. She even visited me in my class, and that people thought that we were dating.

'James!' Babalwa called. That was after school.

Yes!

'I just wanted to talk to you.'

About?

You! To get to know you more better. What you like and what you don't and all that stuff.

Well, I'm not sure about that as well. I don't know what I like and what I don't. I am just me. That's all.

72

'Really!' is there anyone who doesn't know him/herself?

'You're speaking to him. As we speak' I said. I always wanted to tell Babalwa how I felt about her, but I didn't have courage to do that. That's the most painful thing in love. Courage is everything, I mean you need courage to do anything especially in this world of ours. You need to believe in yourself, if you don't, no one will. But I failed to do that. I have several times.

You'll know me soon, you have to know how to study a person. I said to her. I said that on purpose. I know how to study a person, I wanted her to do the same, to learn how to do it.

'Okay then if you say so.'

We were both waiting for our lifts, she was waiting for her father to come and fetch her as I was also waiting for my father as well. She was lucky because sometimes her mother would come and fetch her if her father was busy. I wondered, how it would feel to be fetched from school by your mother.

Is your father coming? I asked.

'It might be my mother.' She said.

Alright! Why are you smiling?

Is your father coming? She asked.

Yes, but I don't know when. He's very busy.

'Alright! Then. Tell me something.'

Something like what? Maybe...

I don't know, something pleasant I guess.

You're beautiful.

We both gave a small laughter.

She was blushing as she was laughing. Arnold and Mihle, our friends were chatting as we were being cozy. They seemed to be so cozy together lately I Arnold didn't tell me anything about what they had, not that he owed me some explanation, but as a friend I needed to know at least if there was something.

'Is that Arnold and Mihle?'

Yes!

'Are they...? You know?'

I should ask you that. Arnold didn't say anything to me. Did Mihle say anything to you, perhaps?

'If she did, do you think I would've asked that question at first?'

You have a point there. But don't mind them. I am sure is nothing serious.

'When are the competitions?

What competitions now?

'Drama competitions...hello! Have you forgotten already?

Oh! That. There are no competitions for me.

'Why?'

I've pulled out. I have a lot on my plate.

'Like hell you do. You can't just pull out now. What! I can't believe this...please James, this is what you wanted to do right? And people have been talking about you in the school.'

'I love acting Babalwa, but I am serious about this, there are many competitions for me, it was the school choir, the acting and the debate still is waiting for me as well.

'I hear you... but still, it doesn't make any sense to me. Does your father support you in your acting path.?

Yes. My father is a supportive man ever.

'What did he say?'

'About you pulling out just like that.'

I didn't say anything.

'What! Did Arnold pull out as well?'

Arnold doesn't know a thing about this. He thinks I am still in.

'Arnold! Arnold!' Babalwa called.

'What are you doing now? I asked.

'Rectifying the situation.' She said.

'Arnold came quickly! What is it?' Arnold asked.

'James has something to tell you.'

'Well what is it? Talk man I'm busy there.'

'She is bluffing Arnold, I have nothing to say.'

'James had pulled out from the acting competition. I was just talking to him to get back there.'

'I was lying Babalwa. Just wanted to see what you are going to do about that.'

Hahah! Arnold and I gave a laughter.

'It's not funny!

'Sorry babe...' I said.

'There's your car Babalwa.' Arnold said.

'Bye-bye guys. See you tomorrow.'

'Sure!' I said.

'Sure? No hug no kiss... nothing?' Arnold contributed.

Babalwa was shy to hear that, on the other side I was shy, and I didn't know what to say. Babalwa left us standing there, looking at each other. She wave over the window. We waved back smiling too.

'Let me go back to Mihle.' Arnold said.

You're not going anywhere. What was that for?

'What? Now?'

That kissing and hugging thing, I am still trying my luck there. Then you became Master of relationships! Besides what is happening between you and Mihle Nkolongo?

'Look man, I am trying my luck too. You do your thing and I do mine as well. Is that clear?'

No! You can't Arnold. We can't date friends.

'Yes we can. It is simple, we are friends, and they are friends too. You like Babalwa, I like Mihle. Finished and klar!'

I am sharing this because it taught me one or two things in life. Firstly Arnold was so stubborn that he wanted things to be as he wished, or as he sees them. Well, nothing is wrong about that, but at least he was supposed to understand my point of view. The reason I am saying this it's because none of it became a reality. Secondly, to me it probably never became a reality because of what I had foreseen. Thirdly, if you cannot get what you want at that particular moment, divert a little bit, try a different method. Remember in math, there are many formulae to calculate the very same sum, some are long, which give more marks and some are short

and even shorter than short but they give the same conclusion. So does life too. We all aim to get somewhere
in the end, but let us look at our methods and formulae of doing things. Some may take the shorter method,
others the longer one. The elders will always say 'the
longer way leads to successes'. Remember I said, the
longer method gives more marks, and at the end, you
would have achieved a lot more through suffering. Note
also that, no one is called to suffer but it's just part of
life. But everyone is called to success because that is our
purpose in life. Look at your method and not of others,
and stick to your lane.

Let's Talk about Umntu

Maybe this will help us to understand that 'Black Lives Matter' and all lives matter too.

Here I seek to bring a comprehensive view on the general existential experience regarding Muntu, or uMntu, according to the Anthropological Philosophy of the Xhosa culture of South Africa. My culture and tribe. This piece of work will first look at the brief history of the anthropological philosophy in the Xhosa culture. Muntu according to the Xhosa culture will be our second topic. We would also entertain their anthropology and social structure. It would be not complete if the language is left behind, hence we shall put an insight on it.

The Xhosa are part of the South African Nguni migration which slowly moved south from the region around the Great Lakes, displacing the original Khoi and the

San, the hunter gatherers of South Africa, as they were famously known. The Xhosa people were established by the time of the Dutch arrival in the mid-17th century, and occupied much of the eastern South Africa from the Fish River to land inhabited by Zulu-speaking south of the modern city of Durban the then the Natal as it was called.

In the years following, many Xhosa-speaking clans were pushed west by expansion of the Zulu, as the northern Nguni put pressure on the southern Nguni as part of the historical process known as the Mfecane, or Difaqane in Sesotho and 'scattering' in simple terms (Qeqe, 2018). The Xhosa-speaking southern Nguni people had initially split into the Gcaleka and the Rharhabe who is believed to have moved westwards across the Kei River, where they had built and formed their anthropological philosophy, having originated in central Africa were they are believed to have come from. The Xhosa tribe has its subdivision, which all have the same anthropological philosophy which is still practiced today.

Further subdivision were made more complicated by the arrival of groups like the Mfengu and the Bhaca from the Mfecane wars. These new comers came to speak the Xhosa language, and are sometimes considered to be Xhosa, although their heritage is still quite distinct. In a way, they have the same philosophy, practice the same cultural customs and practices.

Masculinity studies in South Africa depend on Western gender theories to frame research questions and fieldwork. I come to argue that such theories offer a limited understanding of Xhosa constructions of masculinity. Xhosa notions of masculinity are embodied in the concept of *indoda,* meaning a traditionally circumcised person. This topic explores the nuanced meanings of *indoda* and its relationship to other masculinities, like uncircumcised boys [*inkwenkwe*] and medically circumcised men. The discussion reveals that *indoda* is the most "honoured" form of masculinity. A traditionally circumcised individual is regarded as *indoda,* a real man, irrespective of his sexual orientation or class, and this affords him certain rights and privileges. *Inkwenkwe* and medically circumcised men embody "subordinate" forms of masculinity and are victims of stigma and discrimination by *indoda.* This requires us to revisit some Western theories of masculinity which place heterosexual men at the top of a masculine hierarchy and gay men at the bottom. Ubuntu according to the Xhosa culture is the same like other African cultures. The definition of Ubuntu is simple, it is to do good for another person with famous African saying 'umntu ngumntu ngabanye abantu' - a human being is the human through other human beings. The way Xhosas sees this concept of Ubuntu is not different than any African tribe the way they understand Ubuntu. The Xhosas believed that in life one needs other people and peoples to survive, no person can survive alone (Religion Studies, 2014). This saying Xhosa people takes it practically and literally, for instance if a person is poor in a community the neighbor when is planting something in his garden he will make sure is planting for his poor neighbor as well. In the concept of Ubuntu communal living is encouraged. You share the little that you have, without looking at the color of other person's skin. You simply break the bread and share it with those who need it most.

The famous saying of Bantu people *umntu ngumntu ngabanye abantu* - the person is a person through other human beings, it has deep meaning for people of Bantu. The Bantu people are the people who believe in sharing and helping each other with the spirit of Ubuntu. 'The African teaching of Ubuntu put the community before individual right' (Religion Studies, 2014:3). 'The Bantu sees in man the living force, the force or being that possesses life that is true' (Tempels, 1952:64). Tempels saw a human being as powerful force among other creatures, unlike an animal a man can speak and think. '*Muntu* is force of rational intelligence' (Ledwaba, 2019). It means that a human being can think and capable of reasoning. In other words for a human to be, is to act humanly (Ledwaba, 2019). For Xhosa a human to be *muntu,* must do or act as human being are acting. Xhosa like all other Bantu people they see a human as living force who can relate and share with other people. In my village in the olden days when I was still a young boy, if a man is walking to another village, and night approaches him while still on his way it was a norm that if he wishes he would stop and look around, go to any house he sees and ask for a place to 'hide his head' to sleep in simplest terms and continue with his journey again the following day. He would be then welcomed and feel at home, not like a stranger or foreigner, but as a friend who needed some help. Normally, they would become friends and visit each other again. That is why it was easy to know almost everyone from the nearby villages. All this was the spirit of Ubuntu to welcome any stranger in your house and give him something to eat. The umuntu in the Xhosa culture must be able to live with other people and also be able to welcome all people in his or her house without looking the tribe or color or the standard of living of the visitor. Actually, in the Xhosa culture you can't live alone and be regarded as umuntu or person. That is why we use the saying of "Umntu ngumntu ngabantu." because one needs other people to survive. How can one be known as a person while he or she can't think for his fellow people? When we speak of umuntu who has the spirit of ubuntu, we speak of the person who does not look at the status of a person in order to respect him or her, who will respect everyone. No one can say that he or she does not need other people because he or she has got everything. He can have everything, but he still needs other people because he won't bury himself or carry himself to his grave after his death. In the Xhosa tradition Ubuntu should be attained.

One who lives a communal life through the discharge through one's obligation attains it. Being a person in the Xhosa culture is to be a very important figure because one can do many bad things, they will keep a room for that person hoping that one day he or she will change for the better. We even have a saying, which says, "Umntu akalahlwa." This simply means, there is no bin to throw a person. This means that we should not lose hope in a person. In the Xhosa culture being Umntu is not just a figure, which is taken for granted because the Umuntu should set a good example in his or her community by the life that he or she lives. When one is called Umuntu, he or she is regarded as the disciplined person. By discipline, I mean that one should know what is right and what is wrong to do.

In the community when a person is new, he or she is welcomed by the people and is being ask if he or she needs something and they will offer him some of the things to survive, that's where the person will see the people with the spirit of ubuntu. Ubuntu is taken as part of life. Personhood or being human to other people goes with humbleness. In Africa, personhood has been the part of the culture since from the olden days. According to Ramose personhood is becoming.' He says it is to be in the process of becoming and to be forever becoming. In other words, it does not end until one dies. Living in harmony in the spirit of ubuntu.' Ramose says ubuntu is actually built up in two words ubu and ntu. He says, "ubu- evokes the idea of being in general and ntu is particular." He continues saying that ubuntu or personhood is an indivisible and wholeness. Every person should demonstrate the elements of ubuntu. For example, he or she must be generous and be able to live with other people, rendering services to the community. The man is the one who is given a duty to slaughter a cow, but as we know he cannot do that alone, he needs to be humble and ask other men in the community to come and support him. Even him he has a duty to be human and help the neighbors. He also needs to be humble in thinking the neighbors who helped him in the event. These fulfill the Xhosa saying which says, "Izandla ziyahlambana." This simply means, hands wash each other, that is to say people help one another. Assisting a neighbor is part of being human. It is because one needs the other to make the event successful. Ramose says, "A speech without umuntu, Ubu- is condemned to unbroken silence. The essence of is found in the community."

The normal person knows his philosophy. He knows the operation of the general laws. Usually in the Xhosa world, the elders are the most respected people, because they are the ones who have all the aspects of personhood. Father Ledwaba once said in class, " In the Xhosa culture the death of an older person is like burning the world of experience. This goes in accord with the saying that one becomes a person by listening and obeying the elders. The young ones do not have any experience they have to learn from the elders. To be regarded as Umuntu in the Xhosa culture is something that must be earned, it is not just given to anyone. One has to work for it. We are not denying that we are born human beings, but one has to work hard to be humanely in our actions. A Xhosa is a member of the south-eastern, or Nguni, subgroup of the Bantu group of the Benue-Congo branch of the Niger-Congo language family. Other South-eastern Bantu languages are Zulu, Swati (Swazi), Sotho, Tswana, Venda, and Ndebele. Although Xhosa and Zulu are similar enough to be considered dialects of one language, however, Xhosa and Zulu speakers consider they to be separate languages (Cunningham, 2019)

In South Africa there are 11 official languages, of which Xhosa is one of the most widely spoken languages which was formerly spelled Xosa. It is comes second after IsiZulu as widely spoken. Approximately 16 percent of South Africa's population, or 8.3 million people, cite Xhosa as being their home language. Xhosa is characterised by a number of clicking sounds, which are formed by the tongue. These are represented by the letters c, x and q (Cunningham, 2019). Those that speak the Xhosa language are usually part of an ethnic group known as the amaXhosa. This language is officially referred to as isiXhosa. The word "Xhosa" is derived from the Khoisan language and it means "angry men." Most of the languages in South Africa that involve tongue-clicking originate from the indigenous Khoisan people, who included plenty of different clicks in their speech and language (Cunningham, 2019).

As mentioned before Xhosa falls under the umbrella of the Bantu languages, and is a representative of the south-western Nguni family. As a result, South Africa is known to be the native land of the Xhosa folk. This is especially true of the Eastern Cape, where the language is spoken extensively and taught in the schools of the region. The Zulu people of South Africa have their own name for the Xhosa people, the KwaXhosa. When translated, KwaXhosa simply means "land of Xhosa" (Cunningham, 2019). In the Western Cape and Gauteng province one will also find and hear many Xhosa people. Because Xhosa and Zulu are both classed as Bantu languages, they are quite similar. Therefore, Xhosa and Zulu people frequently understand one another, even if they are each speaking their mother tongue (Cunningham, 2019).

Xhosa has been grouped into several dialects. While the actual dialects are still being finalized, the accepted dialect groups are: Xhosa (original), Gcaleka, Bhaca, Ngqika, Thembu, Mpondomise, Mfengu, Mpondo and Bomvana. Xhosa is an unusual, yet pretty-sounding, language. To many, it is difficult to learn because the consonants are uncommon and also densely populated. The sounds are relatively aggressive (as opposed to soothing and melodic) (Cunningham, 2019).

They comprise English sounds, 15 clicks, ejectives and an implosive. Learners most frequently battle with the

15 clicks, and these are divided into three groups: 1) the dental clicks - where the tongue presses against the person's teeth. The end result should be "tut-tut." 2) Alveolar clicks – where the tongue presses against the palate. The end result should be a sound resembling a cork popping out of a bottle. 3) Lateral clicks - where the tongue presses against the side of the mouth. The end result should be the sound one makes when calling a horse (Cunningham, 2019).

As any with any language, Xhosa had a rich history of oral tradition from which the society taught, informed, and entertained one another. In 1823, the first printing press was set up in the Tyhume Valley. This was made possible by the Scottish Presbyterian missionary, John Bennie, who was also a Xhosa linguist along with John Ross another missionary. The first printed works in Xhosa came out in 1823 from the Lovedale Press in the Alice region of the Eastern Cape. Only in 1859 was the first translation of the Bible printed, which was produced in part by Henry Hare Dugmore (Elphick, Davenport and Davenport, 1997). According to the IsiXhosa culture, as it has been shown above, that it has its roots have been traced from the Khoi and the San people of South Africa, people who were not the same, but the '*same*'. With due regard for this relativity, one may characterize Xhosa Anthropology as intermediate in view of the relativity extensive persistence of features representing affinity with small-scale society in an overall large-scale context. This is probably a transitional phase, but in the light of our present knowledge of societies it is unrealistic to expect a kind of equilibrium in which every trace of the primitive and the small-scale will have disappeared. Again I say, 'Black Lives Matter' and other lives matter too.

Uniting During Crisis

I cannnot think of anything to compare the COVID-19 pandemic but to what is known as the Black Death also known in history as the Black Plague. The Pesstilence was the most fatal pandemic recorded in human history, resulting in the deaths of about 125 million people around the globe.

Like the Black Plague, the Coronavirus probably started in Asia, Central or East. But that is not the case for now, we should not be blaming the people of Asia, especially the Chinese for this current pandemic. We should not call it 'The Chinese Virus', as one Statesman called it. Rather we should be more united because it affects us all. 'Us All', meaning worldwide. It is also time to put aside our indifferences, our hatred for other races or tribes, it is time to see the common in ourselves. What we can all, together and united can archive. This pandemic was first confirmed in late 2019, but it got worse early 2020 to affect negatively the worship of Christians of commemorating The Lord's Supper, The Passion of the Lord, and the brilliant sun of Easter, His Resurrection. Not leaving out the Jewish celebration of the Passover, as it is the great feast to them too.

What can we learn from this? That the world belongs to one God, and we are all His children, whether we believe or not, whether we like it or not. This might also be a challenge in every individual who claims to be a believer. This is a time of prayer for most people, but can we pray now without others? Or we depend on the mass gatherings to pray with others? In the presence of a priests or rabbi? Now it is the time to show that we believe in God, and we are not and we were not pretending. This is the time to revive the world in what I would call, The Renaissance of the Earth. This is the time to come together and be one in all things that affect us all, in all things we have in common. Let us take this opportunity with both hands, to see a good in all what is happening out there, instead of concentrating on the bad side. God probably wants us to be more alert, that we have forgotten about Him, that we have forsaken Him, and that we have put more focus on ourselves as if we a god or something.

For now, let us all stay at home, and be safe. All the Lockdowns in different states, are not to punish people, but to save more lives as much as possible, it is not the time to worry about the economy, planned events or whatever, but to worry about lives that can be saved. Because I, and I am sure, that all would love to travel the world again, because we have tasted that before, and we all know how wonderful it is. Let us keep our children in doors, and have time with them, have time with ourselves. Let us teach them about this pandemic, and how to keep away and safe from it. We always wanted to observe some privacies. This is the time to do that. But we have proven also that we don't want privacy as we claim, because we have proven that wrong, by not obeying the states. Let us obey the government and avoid spreading the virus. This is not to say, 'All South Africans' but 'All peoples of the earth', because we would like to see each other again.

When you feel the Wind you may be sure of the Wind

Before colonization there were no borders in Africa that separated one country from another, as we understand it today. Our kings and chiefs called it regions. But each land was respected by its own culture and language, equally respected. It was thus that permitted people to speak their own mother tongues and remained heard by others of another culture.

We were believers but we worshiped God in our own way, God was never brought by anyone in our continent, but always had been in the center of our lives, respected as the highest being. The mixed marriages that took place in the frontiers of our land, are nothing but a proof that we are a non-violent race that hopes to live in peace with others. We were not educated as the term is comprehended in our times, but yes, we were educated in our own terms hence we could ask our elders to guide and educate us about life. We had no doctors as in the present day, but we lived a healthy life that needed not a medical doctor, but a traditional doctor.

Our skin color was not black nor brown, but African. There was no money but we traded with what we had. We were never rich because no one knows what that means, but yes, we were rich with our own fortune. There was peace, harmony and love among us, but all that was replaced by turmoil and hatred, anger and jealousy and I tell you even corruption dominated. A neighbor was treated like a relative, and not like a stranger.

Africa was treated like the last loaf of bread in the bakery shelf that those who are hungry for it would 'Scramble for Africa'. In the age of time, we were called barbarians, monkeys, and baboons, hottentot and even Niggers and Negros. It was then that we were colonized, and our wealth and resources got looted to build other non-African lands. Because of our skin color, we were tamed to be evil and cruel, inhuman and inferior. Above all in the eyes of the perfect we were a 'freak of nature' that came to existence as a result of a mistake. The aim of the oppressor was to kill and depopulate, so as to ease the process of looting our resources. Intimidation was part of the aim, as to have us spies of the oppressor so that they know the acts of our brothers and sisters who were trying to do good for us all. All these democracies and independences, did not come alone, but unemployment and hunger mounted on us.

All these, poverty and crimes, droughts and corruption are proofs that something went wrong. Our Africaness was polluted and converted even suppressed. We support everything that comes from the West, and even forget about our own. We cry out for help to those who showed no mercy during our times of struggle, because we fear the unknown. Africa is rich in everything, but again we would not rest until we ask for help from the West or Europe. Today we fight against each other's languages and treat them as old school because we have learnt how to speak English properly, even though we cannot, why worry? What went wrong? What changed? We were not using permits to cross borders to those who are neighbors, but we used Bantusm, our existence and appearance. Today we have African Refugees whereas in the past we would have visitors, but also non Africans would be referred to as tourists, while we are refugees.

Why do Africans fight each other, why do they hate each other, why would Africans be more welcoming to non-Africans than Africans? Who is controlling the economy of mother Africa? Who is an investor? Who owns the land in Africa, why Africans migrate to non-African countries? Today we need non-Africans to solve African problems.

I would not have said anything if I don't refer to Ethiopia, who in her troubles managed to keep Africa rising. The defeat of Italy in Ethiopia at the Battle of Adwa is an evidence to this. When you look at the past, you look at Africa being colonized, but watch, Africa colonizing Europe, the Europe of tomorrow. Ethiopia not rising, but Africa rising.

The invention of Ethiopia was too rapid, too precipitately undertaken, everywhere around the world Africans were treated like cattle to be branded with the owners' mark. Italians had been not less courageous or even less enterprising than others but rather made up its mind a little too late. So when they went to Africa to take their share of the fortunes of Africa the easily accessible regions were all been taken up, which left them with no choice, but to touch the untouchable. In all these countries, were news traverses the marshes and the desserts as on the wings of the wind, you may be sure of the wind, you may be sure that, from one part of Africa to another it is already known or it will be so in the near future that Africa has conquered Europe and colonized the Europe of tomorrow. Again, I personally concure with those who continuously emphasize that Africans, and in particular a black child is not going to feed on freedom of speech. Civil Rights is rather a diversion from the main issue. We need in fact fight for the following:

1. Radical Economic Transformation
2. Decolonization of Education &
3. Anthropology of the person and Spirituality.

Africans should and must own the heartbeat of economy and own its vascular, veins and body corporate entirely.

Afterword

Prior colonization, Africa manifested communal life which fostered unity amongst its people in its diversity. Civilization is not a foreign concept to Africans. Furthermore, discrimination was not promoted, everybody was equal hence there was peace, love and harmony amongst Africans. However, jealousy and hatred flourished after colonization and our communal life was eradicated. Africa was independent in every aspect, however on this day and age we depend on those who showed no mercy to Africans as James Qeqe alluded on the last chapter. At the beginning of this Novella, Mthokozisi Mthombeni suggests the slogan 'Africa arise'. We should rise indeed as Africans and maintain our identity while we Foster unity and peace amongst ourselves. The strength and capability of an African is not to be undermined. That is seen in the Battle of

Adwa, when Ethiopia stood and kept Africa rising against the Europeans.

It is a story that should be told, and that The New Voice of Africa should take this as its main objective.

(Sibusiso Mike Zulu, 18th June 2020)

Chief Auditor @ TNVA

List of Reference

Cunningham, J. M. 2019. Xhosa Language. *Encyclopaedia Britannica*. [Online] Available from: https://www.britannica.com/topic/Xhosa-language [cited 07 October 2019]

Elphick, R., Davenport, R. and Davenport, T. R. H. 1997. *Christianity in South Africa: A Political, Social, and Cultural History*. University of California Press.

Ledwaba, T. C. 2019. *African Philosophy*. Pretoria: St John Vianney Seminary. [Unpublished lecture notes].

Qeqe, J. 2018. *The Unknown of the Known in Africa*. Alaska: Publication Constultants.

Wilson, M. & Mafeje, A. 1963. Langa, Cape Town: Oxford Univ. Pr.

Yinger, J. 1957. *Religion, Society and the Individual*. New York: Macmillan.

www.ingramcontent.com/pod-product-compliance
Lightning Source LLC
Chambersburg PA
CBHW07085128O326
41934CB00008B/1401